L'<u>CH</u>AIM: The Jewish Holidays in Rhyme

ISBN: 978-0-9991405-5-0

This book has an audio/visual companion called "The Jewish Holiday Song" and can be found at: **HebrewBasics.com**

L'CHAIM
The Jewish Holidays in Rhyme

- Learn about the Jewish holidays
- Read Hebrew at the bottom of each page
- In the back of the book, you'll find:
  - Explanations of all the Hebrew words in the book
  - A simple guide to the Hebrew letters and vowels
- Find 3 Stars of David in each picture
- The QR code below will take you to the HebrewBasics.com website page with a sing-a-long video using the words from this book

- To learn more, and for more information, visit HebrewBasics.com

These are the Jewish holidays,
we celebrate in so many ways,
coming together to sing and praise,
it's the Jewish year.

Rosh Ha'shana is the new year,
apples and honey, the *shofar* we hear.

Rosh Ha'shana - רֹאשׁ הַשָּׁנָה

Shofar - שׁוֹפָר

Yom Kippur is the holiest day,
ask forgiveness, and *Kol Nidre*.

Yom Kippur - יוֹם כִּפּוּר
Kol Nidre - כָּל נִדְרֵי

We build a *sukkah* on **Sukkot**,
S<u>cha<u>ch (branches) on the roof,
lulav and *etrog*.

---

sukkah - סֻכָּה

Sukkot - סֻכּוֹת

palm branches- סְכָךְ

lulav - לוּלָב

etrog - אֶתְרוֹג

Simchat Torah five books we complete,
dancing, singing in the street.

Simc<u>h</u>at Torah - שִׂמְחַת תּוֹרָה

These are the Jewish holidays,
we celebrate in so many ways,
coming together to sing and praise,
it's the Jewish year.

<u>H</u>anukkah it lasts eight nights,
spin the *dreidel, menorah* we light.

<u>H</u>anukkah - חֲנוּכָּה
Menorah - מְנוֹרָה

Tu B'Shvat is the birthday of the trees,
come and plant, oh won't you please.

Tu B'Shvat - טוּ בִּשְׁבַט

On **Purim** we read *Megillat Esther,*
wear costumes, *Haman* we can't bear.

Purim - פּוּרִים

Megillat Esther - מְגִילַת אֶסְתֵּר

Haman - הָמָן

Pesach, *Seder,*
and *Ma Nishtana,*
We left Egypt eating *Matzah.*

Pesach (Passover) - פֶּסַח

Seder - סֵדֶר

Ma Nishtana - מַה נִּשְׁתַּנָּה

Matzah - מַצָּא

These are the Jewish holidays,
we celebrate in so many ways,
coming together to sing and praise,
it's the Jewish year.

Yom Ha'Zikaron we appreciate,
the soldiers that fought for our Jewish State.

Yom Ha'Zikaron - יוֹם הַזִּכָּרוֹן

Yom Ha'Atzmaut we raise our flag and tell the story of *Medinat Yisrael.*

Yom Ha'Atzmaut - יוֹם הָעַצְמָאוּת
Midinat Yisrael - מְדִינַת יִשְׂרָאֵל

Lag Ba'Omer,

a bonfire we light.

Lag Ba'Omer -לָג בָּעֹמֶר

Shavuot, got the Torah,
Har Sinai!

Shavuot - שָׁבוּעוֹת

Torah - תּוֹרָה

Har Sinai - הַר סִינַי

Tisha B'Av is a very sad day,
Temples destroyed to our dismay.

Tisha B'Av - תִּשְׁעָה בְּאָב

These are the Jewish holidays,
we celebrate in so many ways,
coming together to sing and praise,
it's the Jewish year.

But perhaps our most special holiday,
is the one that comes every week,
HOORAY!
It's a family time with *<u>ch</u>allah* and wine,
and it starts on Friday night.

_____

<u>Ch</u>allah - חַלָּה

Shabbat Shalom is what we say,
we see each other throughout the day.
A day of peace and a day of rest,
so that everyone feels blessed.

Shabbat Shalom - שַׁבָּת שָׁלוֹם

THE END
הַסוֹף

Keep reading to learn more…

Hebrew words on each holiday* page:

Rosh Hashana - New Year (literally "head of the year")

Shofar - a ram's horn we blow (and sound) to announce the new year

Yom Kippur - Day of Atonement

Kol Nidre - the opening *t'filla* (prayer) of *Yom Kippur*

Sukkot - Holiday of Booths

Sukkah - a temporary dwelling (booth) we build

Schach - the palm leaves, or other natural material, placed on the roof of the *sukkah*

Lulav - A palm branch (coupled with Myrtle and Willow branches.)

Etrog - A unique citron fruit, similar to a lemon

Simchat Torah - The day we celebrate completing the yearly reading cycle of the Torah

Torah - The five books of *Moshe* (Moses)

Hanukkah - Rededicate (Rededicated the *Beit Hamikdash* (Holy Temple) after the Maccabean victory over the Syrian-Greeks.)

Dreidel - Yiddish word for a spinning top In Hebrew, it's called a *Siveevon*

Menorah - A lamp or candleabra On *Hanukkah*, we light an eight-branched menorah called a *Hanukkiah*

Tu B'Shvat - 15th day (in the Hebrew month) of Shvat

*Holiday names are in bold

Purim - lots, as in a lottery   (We celebrate the story of Esther)

Megillat Esther - The scroll of Esther (The story of Purim is written upon it)

Haman - The villain in the story of *Purim*

Pesach - pass over (G-d passed over Jewish homes as they left Egypt from enslavement)

Seder - order (The name of the festive meal that we eat on *Pesach*)

Ma Nishtana - What is different (on this night) (A song during the *seder*)

Matzah - unleavened bread we eat on *Pesach*

Yom Ha'Zikaron - Memorial Day

Yom Ha'Atzmaut - Independence Day

Medinat Israel - The State of Israel

Lag Ba'Omer - 33rd day of the Omer*

Shavuot - weeks (Culmination of 7 weeks from Pesach to Shavuot)

Har Sinai - Mount Sinai (Location where the Jews
              received the Torah)

Ti'sha B'Av - 9th day (in the Hebrew month) of *Av*

Shabbat - Sabbath (the day of rest)

Challah - a special bread we eat on *Shabbat*

Shabbat Shalom - peaceful Sabbath

Shalom - hello, goodbye, peace

*The *Omer* is a daily counting of the days between the holidays of *Pesach* and *Shavuot*

The Printed Hebrew Alphabet, the "*Aleph-Bet,*" and the Vowels

Hebrew reads right to left.

←אבגדהוזחטיכלמנסעפצקרשת

The vowels are symbols found under (sometimes on top of or next to) the letters:

֭ – ֲ = "a" as in <u>a</u>qua

ֱ ֵ = "e" as in r<u>e</u>d

֗ = "ee" as in gr<u>ee</u>n

וֹ = "o" as in <u>o</u>range

וּ ֻ = "oo" as in bl<u>ue</u>

ִ = "i" as in <u>i</u>ndigo

The letters sound like the first letter in their name:

La'med	ל	Aleph	א
Mem	מ	Bet/Vet	ב
Noon	נ	Gimmel	ג
Sameh	ס	Dalet	ד
Ayin	ע	Hay	ה
Pay/Fay	פ	Vav	ו
Tzadi	צ	Zayin	ז
Koof	ק	<u>Het</u>	ח
Reish	ר	Tet	ט
Shin/Sin	ש	Yud	י
Tav	ת	Kaf/<u>H</u>af	כ

To learn more, visit HebrewBasics.com

Learn more with additional books and games by Michelle Geft:

<u>Read, Write, Recite Hebrew</u>
- teaches how to read the printed alphabet with vowels
and to write the script letters

<u>Read Hebrew!</u>
- teaches how to read the printed alphabet with vowels (no script letters)

<u>The Aleph Bet Coloring Book</u>
- teaches the alphabet and vowels
(Designed for younger learners, but adults love it too!)

<u>Shalom Israel</u>
- teaches conversational Hebrew through a modern Israel connection

"Roll n' Learn Hebrew: Not Your Classic Dice Game"
- teaches Hebrew letters, gematria, math and more!

Available on Amazon.com and/or HebrewBasics.com